STEP-UP Books

are written especially for children who have outgrown beginning readers. In this exciting series:

- the words are harder (but not too hard)
- there's more text (but it's still in big print)
- there are plenty of illustrations (but the books aren't picture books)
- the subject matter has been carefully chosen to appeal to young readers who want to find out about the world around them. They'll love these informative and lively books.

SEA CREATURES DO AMAZING THINGS

Have you ever seen

- a left-handed lobster?
- a dancing crab?
- a 500-pound clam?

This carefully researched book is filled with astonishing and little-known information about these and more than a dozen other animals that live in the sea. Arthur Myers' fascinating stories about sea creatures make fact as entertaining as fiction.

Sea Creatures Do

by Arthur Myers   illustrated by Jean Day Zallinger

Amazing Things

Step-Up Books ⌐ Random House
New York

Library of Congress Cataloging in Publication Data:
Myers, Arthur (date). Sea creatures do amazing things. (Step-up books) SUMMARY: Discusses the octopus, paper nautilus, sponge, sea cucumber, giant clam, starfish, sea anemone, jellyfish, corals, barnacles, and other unusual sea creatures. 1. Marine fauna—Juvenile literature. [1. Marine animals] I. Zallinger, Jean Day. II. Title. QL122.2.M93 591.92 80-20089 ISBN: 0-394-84487-4 (trade); 0-394-94487-9 (lib. bdg.)

Manufactured in the United States of America   6 7 8 9 0

Contents

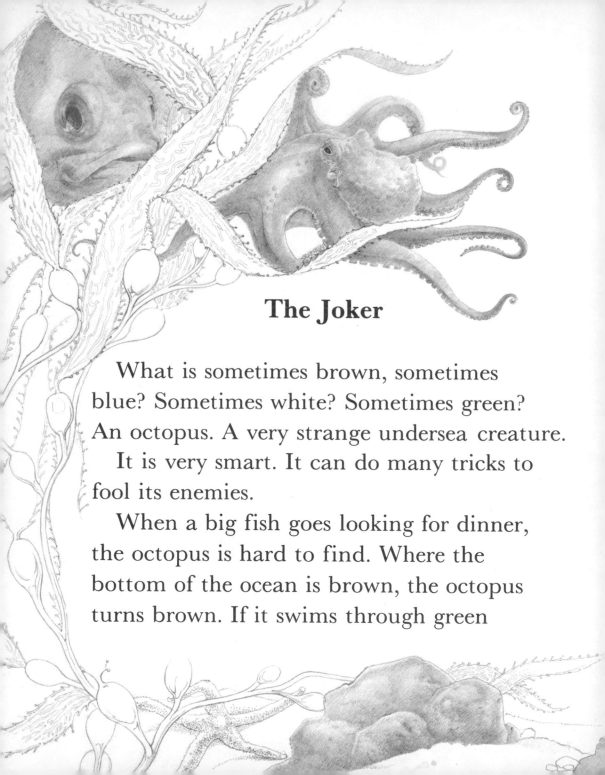

The Joker

What is sometimes brown, sometimes blue? Sometimes white? Sometimes green? An octopus. A very strange undersea creature.

It is very smart. It can do many tricks to fool its enemies.

When a big fish goes looking for dinner, the octopus is hard to find. Where the bottom of the ocean is brown, the octopus turns brown. If it swims through green

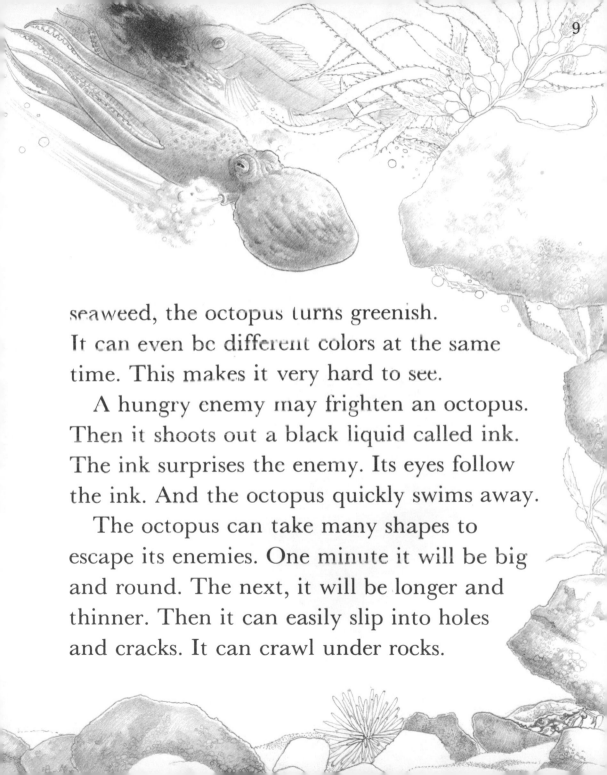

seaweed, the octopus turns greenish.
It can even be different colors at the same
time. This makes it very hard to see.

A hungry enemy may frighten an octopus.
Then it shoots out a black liquid called ink.
The ink surprises the enemy. Its eyes follow
the ink. And the octopus quickly swims away.

The octopus can take many shapes to
escape its enemies. One minute it will be big
and round. The next, it will be longer and
thinner. Then it can easily slip into holes
and cracks. It can crawl under rocks.

The octopus likes to make its home under rocks. But many other things will do. Near the shore it finds bottles, cans, old tires. These are great places for an octopus to live. A sunken ship can become an apartment house for octopuses. A ship has so many hiding places.

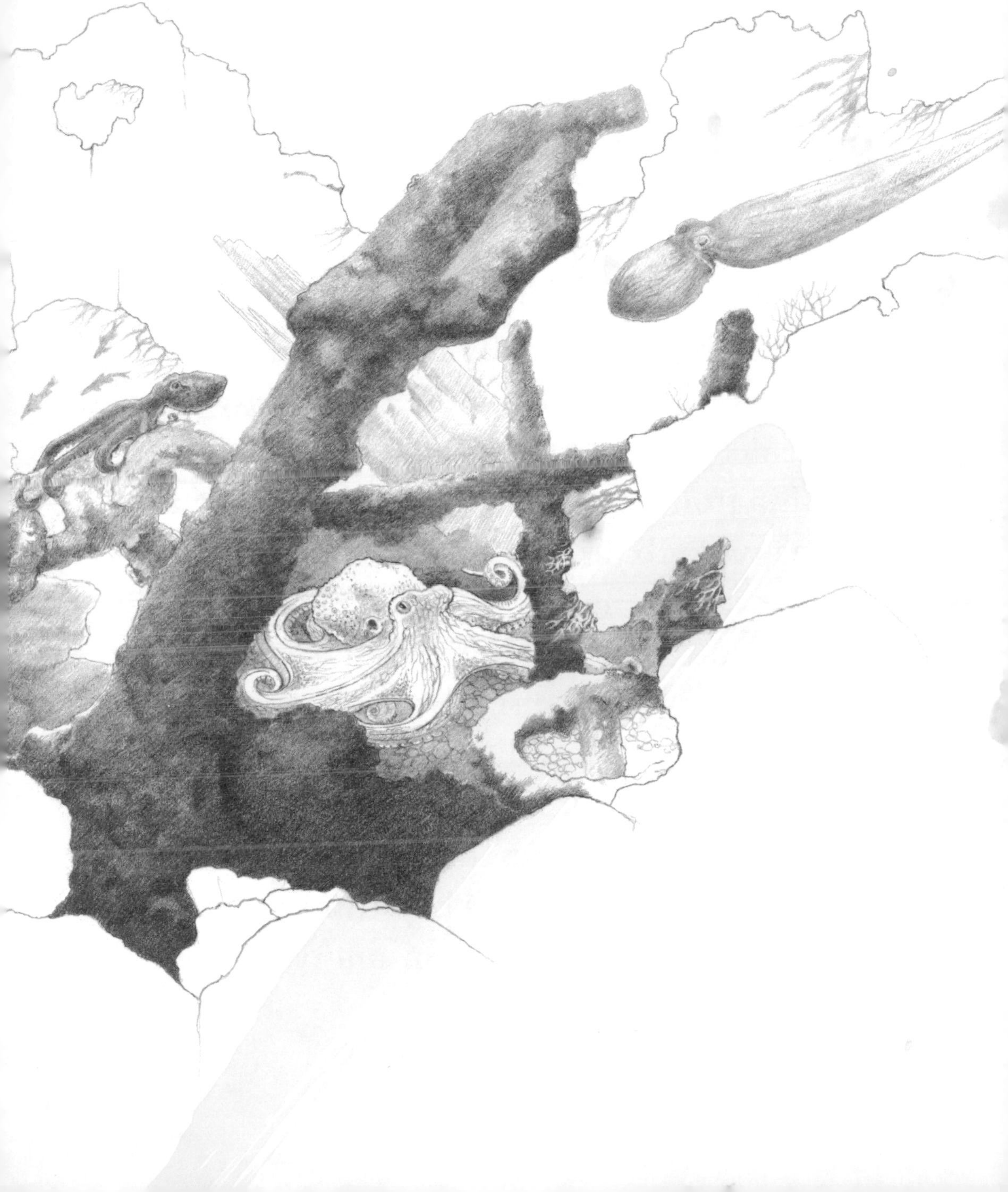

Octopuses like to play jokes. In an aquarium, they will squirt water at people. Sometimes they pull the plugs in their tanks. And the water runs out.

Octopuses can be found in almost all the oceans. They are usually near the shore. There are nearly 150 kinds. And many sizes. Some octopuses in the ocean off the state of Washington are giants. Their bodies are as big as basketballs. Their arms can spread ten feet (three meters). But some of their cousins in the South China Sea are midgets. Their bodies are the size of golf balls.

Octopuses are good to eat. When you chew one, you will find that it feels very rubbery. Some people think that is because its body **is** like rubber. They think that is why an octopus can take on many shapes.

But they are wrong. An octopus can change its shape because it has no bones. When you finish eating octopus, there is nothing left to feed your dog!

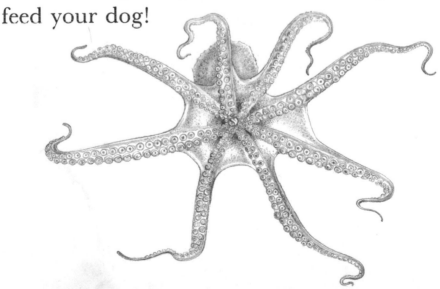

The Sailboat That Isn't a Sailboat

The paper nautilus (NAWT-uh-luss) had people fooled for many, many years.

Sailors and fishermen in warm seas sometimes saw a shell moving along the water. It was beautiful. It looked like the sail of a tiny sailboat. But it was really the shell of a sea creature.

This creature looked like a little octopus. It had eight arms and a very thin shell. It held up this shell like a sail.

People called this strange creature the paper nautilus. They named it the nautilus because that means little sailor in Greek. They called it paper because its shell was as thin as paper.

We know today that the nautilus is not using its shell as a sail. A sailboat is blown along by the wind. But the nautilus moves along much like a ship with a jet engine. A jet plane sends out hot gases in one direction. The plane moves in the other direction. The nautilus takes in water. Then it squirts the water out through a tube under its head. This stream moves in one direction. It pushes the nautilus in the other direction.

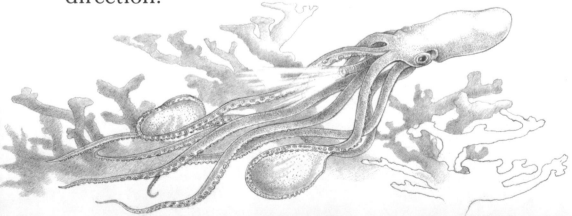

If the thin shell of the nautilus is not a sail, what is it? It is really an egg cradle. It is carried by the female. Two of her arms are shaped like fans. From them comes a thick liquid. When it dries, it forms part of a shell. Little by little the female builds a whole shell. She then puts her eggs in the shell. It will keep them safe.

The nautilus is not attached to the shell. She can drop it at any time. But she does not do so until her eggs hatch. The next year she makes another shell for her new eggs.

The male nautilus does not make a shell.
In fact, the male was something of a mystery
until modern times. Scientists now know
that he is very small. He is much, much
smaller than the female. He may be only
one inch (25 millimeters) long. She may be
ten times his size. But she needs him to lay a
thick liquid on top of her eggs. Then the
eggs will be fertilized (FUR-tuh-lized). And
soon new paper nautiluses will be born.

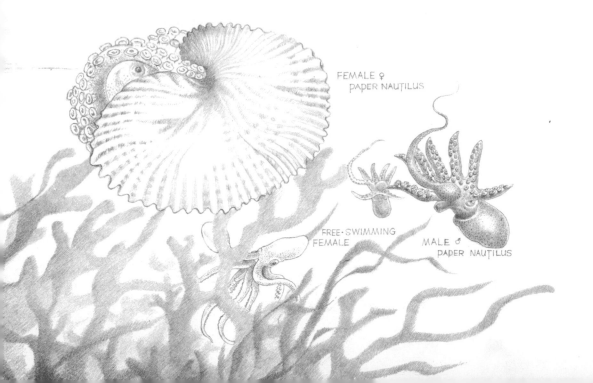

FEMALE ♀
PAPER NAUTILUS

FREE-SWIMMING
FEMALE

MALE ♂
PAPER NAUTILUS

It's Hard to Kill a Sponge

Most people think of sponges as something for washing the car or the windows. But sponges are really animals that grow under the water. They can be found in the salty sea, or in fresh-water lakes.

They are very simple animals. They are so simple that for many years people thought they were plants. They do not move around. They have no heart, no lungs, no brain. But they must be doing something right. For sponges have been around for hundreds of millions of years.

Sponges can be as small as a bean. Or bigger than a barrel. Some are six feet (nearly two meters) high. They have all kinds of shapes. They can look like hoses or pots. Or like nothing but blobs. They have many colors. They can be bright red or yellow. They can be pink, or blue, or purple.

A sponge lives by taking in water through small openings. These openings are on the outside of its body. In this water are tiny animals and plants. The water flows through hollow tubes in the sponge's body. Thousands of them. Many of the little animals and plants become food for the sponge.

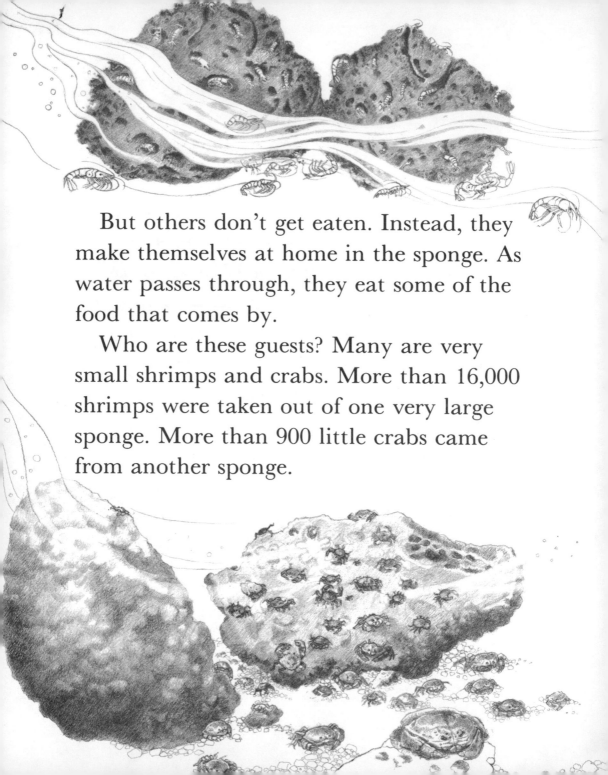

But others don't get eaten. Instead, they make themselves at home in the sponge. As water passes through, they eat some of the food that comes by.

Who are these guests? Many are very small shrimps and crabs. More than 16,000 shrimps were taken out of one very large sponge. More than 900 little crabs came from another sponge.

Sponges are very hard to kill. Tear a sponge into two pieces. You will have two living sponges. Break a sponge into a hundred pieces. You will have a hundred

sponges. Some scientists believe that is because a sponge is not just one animal. They say that each hollow tube is a whole animal. So one sponge is really thousands of animals that live together!

The Sea Cucumber's Funny Tricks

Some sea cucumbers have a very strange way of getting away from their enemies. Their trick will really surprise you. When a sea cucumber is attacked, it squirts out parts of its insides. "Here," it seems to be saying to its attacker. "Here is something for you to eat."

While the other animal is busy eating the cucumber's insides, the rest of the cucumber gets away. In a few days, it will regrow the parts it lost.

This trick does not work when people are the cucumber's enemies. Divers gather them from the bottom of the sea where they live. Then the cucumbers become food for humans. Some Asians eat them dried and smoked, or in soup.

Sea cucumbers don't taste like vegetable cucumbers. They got their name because they are shaped like vegetable cucumbers. But the two tastes are **very** different. After all, cucumbers are plants. Sea cucumbers are animals.

These animals can be as long as five feet (more than one meter). Or as short as a few inches. Some are pink or violet. Others are red, orange, or brown. They live at the bottom of oceans over most of the world.

Sea cucumbers are sometimes fat and sometimes skinny. Their thickness depends on how much they ate and drank that day.

They drink water. They eat tiny plants and animals they find on the floor of the sea. These little creatures are mixed in the mud on the sea floor. Sea cucumbers also eat tiny animals that swim by.

A sea cucumber has short, thick feelers. They look a little like fingers. These feelers scoop mud into the cucumber's mouth. The feelers also wave around through the water. They are sticky. So little animals get stuck to them. Then the cucumber licks its "fingers" like a boy or girl eating jam.

Some sea cucumbers have another strange trick. When they are scared, they break themselves in two. This confuses whatever animal is attacking them. The two parts can get away. Then each part grows the half that is missing. Instead of being some other animal's dinner, the cucumber is now two cucumbers.

Bursting Out

Can you imagine growing out of your bones? If you were a lobster, it could happen. For a lobster's skeleton is on the outside of its body. The skeleton is called a shell.

The lobster grows until it bursts its shell. When the shell cracks the lobster crawls out. A new shell has grown under the old one. This new shell is soft. But after a while it becomes hard.

The lobster keeps growing new shells all

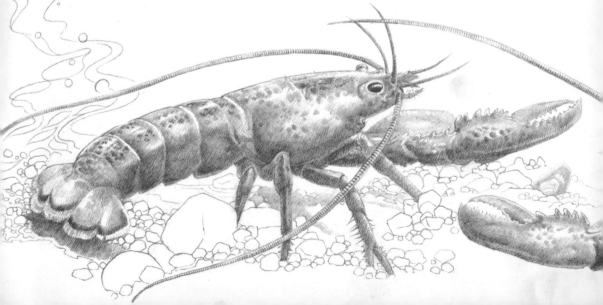

its life. During its first year, it grows six or eight shells. Later it does this once or twice a year. Scientists think some lobsters live as long as fifty years. Think of all the shells it has gone through!

The lobster crawls along the bottom of the ocean. It looks for food. Dinner can be fish, crabs, tiny animals. Even another lobster! The lobster isn't very fussy about what it eats.

The lobster itself makes a fine meal for people. Fishermen use wooden traps to catch the lobsters. The fishermen put fish in the traps. Then they lower the traps into the water. Lobsters crawl in to get the fish. But they can't get out again. They end up as somebody's dinner.

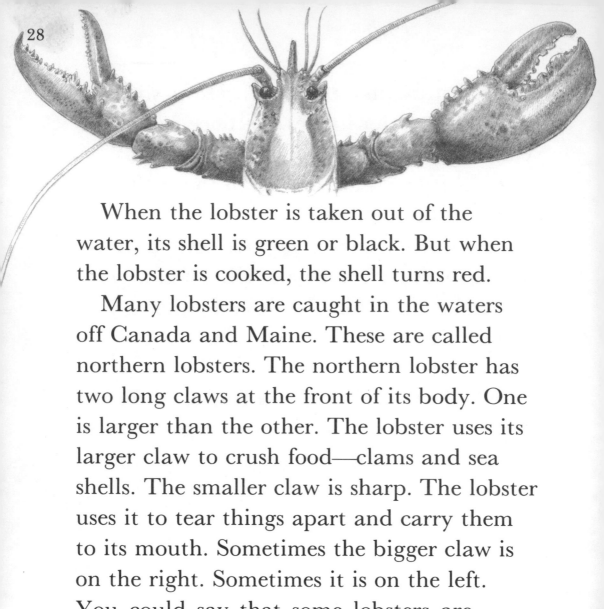

When the lobster is taken out of the water, its shell is green or black. But when the lobster is cooked, the shell turns red.

Many lobsters are caught in the waters off Canada and Maine. These are called northern lobsters. The northern lobster has two long claws at the front of its body. One is larger than the other. The lobster uses its larger claw to crush food—clams and sea shells. The smaller claw is sharp. The lobster uses it to tear things apart and carry them to its mouth. Sometimes the bigger claw is on the right. Sometimes it is on the left. You could say that some lobsters are right-handed. Others are left-handed.

Most of the time, a lobster stays by itself. But now and then it finds a mate. Mating time is right after a female sheds her shell. Several months later the female lays eggs. Sometimes she lays 150,000 of them! From these eggs come baby lobsters.

Most of them grow to be about a foot (30 centimeters) long. But sometimes lobsters grow to almost three times that size. A lobster this big can weigh almost 50 pounds (about 23 kilograms)! What a meal!

The Biggest Clam in the World

If you think a 50-pound lobster is big,
how about a 500-pound clam! A clam like
this could be long enough for you to lie
down on. Most clams could fit in your hand.
It takes about four of them to weigh one
pound (less than a kilogram).

The giant clams are found in the Pacific Ocean near Australia and in the Indian Ocean. One such clam can be a feast for a big party of people. It can have 20 pounds (9 kilograms) or more of meat.

Sometimes people use the shells of these clams as wash basins. The shells also make good baby bathtubs.

There are many stories about how dangerous giant clams are to people. The stories say divers can get their legs or arms caught in the clam. Then the person will drown. But these stories are probably not true. For the giant clam closes its shell very slowly. A person would almost have to be trying to get caught. Besides, these huge clams eat only tiny plant life.

Clams can make pearls—the way oysters do. Giant clams sometimes have pearls as big as golf balls!

The Stomach That Crawls After Food

Did you ever try to open a clam with your fingers? If you did try, I'll bet you did not get the clam open. Even a very strong man could not pull a clam's shell apart. For the clam can hold its shell closed very tightly.

Yet the starfish opens clams all the time. Clams are the starfish's favorite food. And most starfish are not much bigger than small clams.

Starfish are found in all the oceans of the world. They often can be seen along the shore. So can clams. Many of both creatures can be found along the coasts of North America.

How does the starfish open a clam that does not want to be opened? The starfish simply climbs around the clam. The starfish has little suckers on its arms. The suckers stick to the clam's shell. Then begins a tug-of-war. The starfish tries to open the clam. The clam tries to stay closed.

Sometimes this game of life or death goes on for hours. But the starfish almost always wins. The clam weakens, and its shell opens a little.

Then an amazing thing happens. The starfish's stomach comes out of its mouth. The stomach slides through the opening in the clam's shell. Before long, the stomach has eaten the soft body of the clam. Then the starfish pulls its stomach back into its own body.

It's one of the world's strangest ways of eating.

The Dangerous Flower

The sea anemone (uh-NEM-uh-nee) looks like a flower. It is even named after a land flower, the anemone. But most sea anemones don't look like anemone flowers. Instead, they look like other flowers—mostly dahlias (DAL-yuz) or chrysanthemums (krih-SAN-thuh-mumz).

CHRYSANTHEMUM   DAHLIA

Yet the sea anemone is not a flower. It is not even a plant. It is a beautiful sea animal.

It may be blue, green, pink, or red. Sometimes the same anemone has many colors. Some are striped.

The anemone has a stalk like a flower. At the top of the stalk are feelers. They look something like the petals of a flower. But these long, thin feelers are dangerous. They have poison needles.

If a small fish swims too close to the anemone, the feelers grab it. They shoot poison into the fish. The anemone then pulls the fish into its mouth. A fine supper.

The anemone's poison feelers are a help to some sea creatures. One of these is the pretty little striped clown fish. The anemone's poison does not hurt the clown fish. So the clown fish hides among the anemone's feelers. Other creatures do not dare attack the clown fish there.

Some hungry crabs use the sea anemone as a poisoned knife. The anemone's poison does not hurt these crabs. A crab holds an anemone in its claw and stabs a passing animal. Then the crab has the animal for dinner.

Hermit crabs also use anemones. But in a different way. These crabs decorate their shells with anemones. The bottom of an anemone's stalk is like a sucker. A hermit crab sticks the end of a stalk to its shell. Then the crab cannot easily be seen by its enemies.

Normally, an anemone sticks itself to a rock. Or it sticks to the wood of a dock. Then it usually stays there.

It can loosen itself and move if it wants to. And sometimes it does. But it moves very slowly. Hours go by before it moves one inch!

The anemone has three different ways of making new anemones. Sometimes it lays eggs. Sometimes it splits itself in two. Each half becomes a new anemone. Other times it just leaves parts of itself around. This can happen when it makes a move. It may leave a dozen little pieces of itself on the rock it was stuck to. Each piece becomes a new anemone.

The Animals People Live On

How big do you have to be to build an island? Not very big. The tiny sea animals called corals build islands big enough for people to live on. Yet some corals are no bigger than a pinhead.

We humans have our bones, or skeletons, on the inside of our bodies. But the coral builds its skeleton around the outside of its soft body. Each little skeleton is shaped like a cup. Many, many corals live together. And their skeletons stick together.

After a time, the animals die. But the hard, bony cups remain. New coral animals attach themselves to the old skeletons. Later, the new animals die too. But their skeletons remain. After hundreds of years, the skeletons are piled up. Sometimes they are hundreds of feet high. They look and feel like rock.

Such a mass of coral is called a coral reef. You can see one if you dive in the warm oceans of the world. Or you can take a trip in a glass-bottomed boat. Then you can see the reef and never even get wet.

The coral reef may poke above the surface of the sea. It sometimes becomes covered with earth. Trees grow there. People and animals can live on this coral island.

If you look at coral rock closely, you will see tiny holes. Each hole is where a coral animal stuck out the tip of its soft body, searching for food. It had little feelers, with poison tips. It stung animals even smaller than itself. Then it drew the animals into its body, for food.

Coral rock can be different colors. Sometimes it is white like bone. Sometimes it is pink, or even deep red. Some coral rock is black.

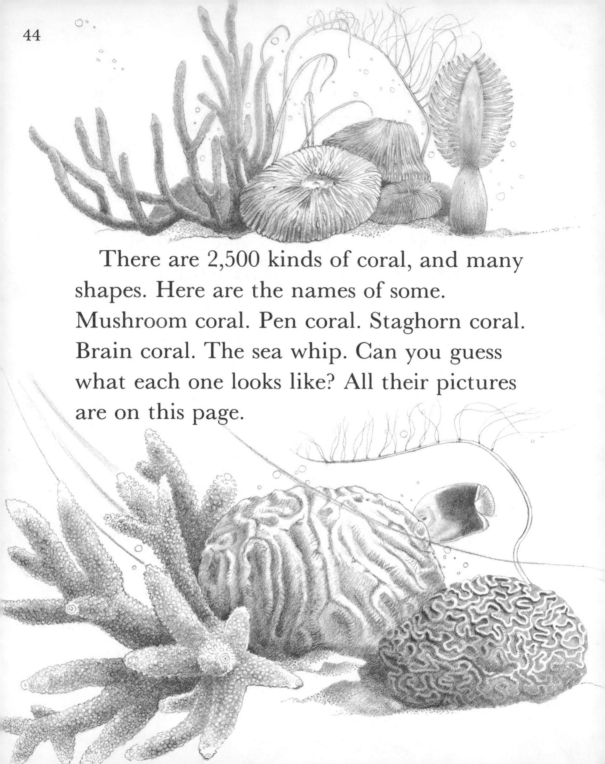

There are 2,500 kinds of coral, and many shapes. Here are the names of some. Mushroom coral. Pen coral. Staghorn coral. Brain coral. The sea whip. Can you guess what each one looks like? All their pictures are on this page.

The Dancing Crab

Picture a crab that dances. Not only that, it seems to be playing the fiddle. Fiddle is another word for violin. This talented crab is the fiddler crab. You can see how it gets its name.

The male fiddler crab plays and dances for love. He wants to attract a female fiddler crab. During the mating season he turns beautiful colors. His back may be white and blue. Or it can turn green or purple. His eight legs may be bright red.

The male fiddler crab has two claws. They are very different. One is small. He uses it for eating. But the other! Ah, that is **some** claw. If you use your imagination, the big claw looks like a fiddle. And the smaller claw looks like a bow. A bow is a long stick. A violin player draws it across the violin to make music.

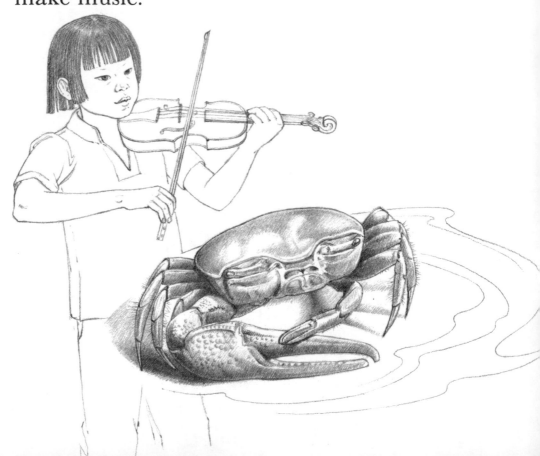

At mating time, the big claw turns pink, or purple, or bright red. The crab waves this claw at a female. Some kinds of fiddlers wave their claw up and down. Some kinds wave it sideways. Some kinds wave it in circles.

While the male waves his claw, he dances. He turns around so the female can see him.

Some male crabs also make sounds to attract the female. They do this by rubbing the rough parts of their legs together. Some sound as though they are singing.

Fiddler crabs live at the edge of the sea. Their lives are affected by how high or low the water is. Sometimes the water is high. It comes far up on the shore. This is called high tide. Sometimes the water is low. It does not come very far onto the shore. This is called low tide.

Fiddler crabs dig holes in the sand. These holes are called burrows. The crabs stay in their burrows when the tide is high. For they cannot swim. When the water covers their burrows, it traps air inside. The crabs breathe these bubbles of air.

When the tide is low, the fiddlers go out. They look for something to eat. Or males wave their big, beautiful claws at passing females. The crabs' color is pale in their burrows. But when they go out, they turn darker.

Fiddler crabs always know if the tide is high or low. Some crabs knew this in a tank hundreds of miles from the sea. When the tide was low, their color grew darker. They moved around more. They seem to have some kind of clock in their bodies that says, "High tide! Low tide!"

The Crab That's Not a Crab

When is a crab not a crab? When it's a horseshoe crab. For a horseshoe crab is not a real crab.

It looks like a big crab. It has a hard, flat shell. It acts like a crab, the way it crawls along. But it is really a relative of the spider. Yet the horseshoe crab is not like a spider, either. It is different from any other animal.

One kind of horseshoe crab lives along the East Coast of North America. Sometimes you can find its shell on beaches. Four other kinds live in waters off Japan and India.

Horseshoe crabs have been on earth for a very long time. Some scientists say as long as 300 million years. They were here before the dinosaurs. And of course long after. Most animals keep changing as time goes by. After a few million years they look very different. But the horseshoe crab has changed very little. It looks almost the same as it always has.

How does the horseshoe crab get its name? If you turned it over, it would look a lot like a horseshoe with a tail. Sometimes the crab gets turned on its back. Then it uses its long, strong tail to turn itself over. That tail is a very handy thing to have.

The American Indians thought so too. They used this stiff, sharp tail as a tip for their spears.

The Porcupine of the Sea

Imagine a sea creature that looks like a pincushion. This is the sea urchin. Sometimes it is called the porcupine of the sea. It has sharp spines like a porcupine.

If you see a sea urchin on the beach, don't touch it. Those spines may break off in your hand. That is how they protect the sea urchin from its enemies.

The sea urchin eats mostly dead animals and dead plants. But urchins also eat live seaweed and small live animals. They find this live food on rocks and on the sea bottom.

The urchin has a handy way of eating. Its mouth is on the bottom of its body. So it does not have to stop moving to have dinner. The urchin chews as it crawls along. It looks like a moving pincushion.

The sea urchin has five teeth. They are both sharp and strong. They can even bite into soft rock.

Such teeth serve some sea urchins well. Most urchins bury themselves in sand at the edge of the sea. But some make holes in rock and live in the holes. These urchins use their teeth to dig the hole. Their little feet help in digging too.

The sea urchin has many tiny feet to walk on. Some urchins also walk on their spines. These are urchins that have long and thick spines. They do not go very fast, but they are funny to watch. They look like they are walking on stilts.

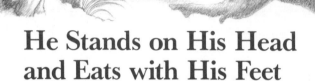

He Stands on His Head and Eats with His Feet

Barnacles are great at grabbing free rides. You can find them on the bottoms of ships sailing through the sea. The barnacles glue themselves to fish, turtles, or whales. Once they get on, they never get off. They even stick themselves to the bottoms of seaplanes. Up they go into the sky!

But most barnacles stay in one place. If you go down to almost any ocean shore, you will find barnacles. Billions and billions of them! They also live deep in the sea. Some barnacles live more than three miles (nearly 11 kilometers) down.

There are almost 1,000 different kinds of barnacles. They come in many sizes. Some are so small you can hardly see them. A few are as big as a large grapefruit.

They have many shapes. A common sort is the acorn barnacle. It looks like an acorn nut. The goose barnacle has a long neck like a goose.

Most barnacles have hard shells. The shell protects the soft body inside. The barnacle opens its shell at the top when it wants to eat. It sticks out curly little feelers. These feelers sweep through the water like feathers. They brush tiny animals into the barnacle's mouth.

You can see why a famous scientist once described the barnacle in this way: "It is an animal that stands on its head in a stone house. And when it gets hungry, it kicks food into its mouth."

When the barnacle is first born, it is almost too tiny to see. It is soft and has no shell. It swims around. It eats, and it grows. Sometimes it is eaten by bigger things in the sea.

HOW A BABY BARNACLE GROWS UP

As it grows, it changes its looks. It grows a hard shell. Most of its head disappears. Its swimming legs stick up through the top of the shell. They turn into the feelers that it uses for eating.

One of the strangest changes is in the barnacle's eyes. It starts life with one eye. Then it grows two more. That makes three. As an adult, it sheds the last two. That leaves one again. In some barnacles, this one eye splits into two eyes.

As an adult, it stops swimming. It attaches itself to something. Its new home can be a rock, a log, a ship, or a fish. Almost anything solid will do.

The barnacle stays there for the rest of its life. It is very hard to pull loose. For the glue it makes is probably the best in the world.

Living Jewels

One of the most beautiful of tiny creatures is the diatom (DYE-uh-tum). Diatoms come in all colors and many, many shapes. Some are as small as a speck of dust. Others are as long and wide as this line —.

Diatoms can look like circles, or squares, or spools. They can look like toothpicks, flying saucers, or footballs. Think of almost any shape. You can find a diatom that looks like it.

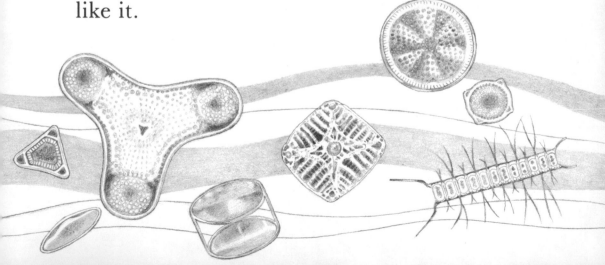

Diatoms are so pretty that people used to
collect them. They dried them and put them
on glass slides. Then they looked at the
slides under a microscope. One famous slide
holds more than four thousand diatoms.
Men used to give ladies slides of diatoms.
For diatoms are like living jewels.

Diatoms are not animals; they are plants. They have been called the grasses of the sea. They are called this because many tiny animals eat diatoms. These animals are in turn eaten by larger ones. So the diatom is the start of nature's chain of food.

The diatom floats in the water. It usually stays near the surface, to catch the rays of the sun. Some diatoms can move by themselves. Most just go along with the movement of the water. Sometimes they float alone. But sometimes they stick to other diatoms. This may cause a yellow or brown slick on the water. This carpet of diatoms can reach for hundreds of miles.

Because diatoms are plants, they give off oxygen (OCK-sih-jun). This helps animals, including humans, to breathe. For animals need oxygen. Diatoms put a lot of oxygen into the air.

Even though the diatom is so tiny, it has a shell. It makes its shell out of the silicon it finds in the sea. Silicon is much like sand. It is hard and tough. When the diatom dies, the shell stays behind. It may sink to the bottom of the sea. Sometimes it becomes part of the land. Much land is built out of the shells of diatoms.

The Water Balloons

They look like balloons as they float along on the water. Or maybe like umbrellas. Or soup bowls that have been turned upside down.

They are called jellyfish. Because their insides are very soft, like jelly.

If you dived under them, you would see thin arms hanging down. These arms look something like spaghetti. They are called tentacles (TEN-tuh-kulz). Some jellyfish have a few tentacles. Some have hundreds. Some tentacles are long. Some are short.

The tentacles of most jellyfish are dangerous. A jellyfish uses its tentacles to catch food. Once it holds a fish, it stings the fish with poison. Then the fish cannot swim. And the jellyfish eats it.

All jellyfish will sting humans who get too close. This can be very painful. If you see a jellyfish washed up on the beach, don't touch it. It might not be the poisonous kind. But it could be.

Man-of-War

The Portuguese (pour-chuh-GEEZ)
man-of-war looks like a jellyfish. But it isn't.
In fact it's not one animal at all. It is a
group of hundreds of animals that live
together. Within the group are four different
kinds of animals. Each kind has its own job.

The kind you see on top of the water is a large bag of gas. It can be bright blue, or red, or green. It is so bright it is hard to miss. Its job is to keep all the others floating.

Under it hang animals of a second kind. They are in the form of tentacles. They are often many yards long. And they sting. Their job is to catch food.

Right under the gas bag is a third kind of animal. All this animal does is eat. It eats for itself and the other kinds of animals that make up the man-of-war. The tentacle brings the food up to the eating animal. If the piece of food is small, this animal swallows it. If it is a large fish, many men-of-war share it. Sometimes they completely cover the fish as they eat.

The fourth kind of animal in the man-of-war is there just to make babies.

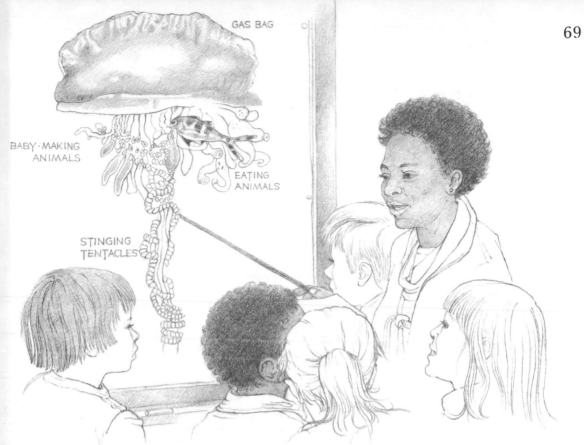

Each Portuguese man-of-war has both male
and female of this kind. With the other
kinds of animals, they live under the gas
bag, and do their job.

They all get along very well, helping each
other live. We humans could learn a lot
from the Portuguese man-of-war.

ABOUT THE AUTHOR AND ILLUSTRATOR

Arthur Myers has spent many years as a newspaper man, magazine editor, writer, and teacher of writing. Recently he has been concentrating on creating books especially for young readers. So far he has had over a half-dozen published, including another Step-Up, *Kids Do Amazing Things*. Mr. Myers was born and raised in Buffalo, New York. For the past 23 years, he has made his home in the Berkshire Hills of western Massachusetts.

Art is everywhere in the life of **Jean Zallinger**. Not only is she the illustrator of about 60 books, including four award winners and the recent Random House book *Nature's Champions*, but she is an associate professor at the Paier School of Art in Hamden, Connecticut. She is married to painter Rudolph Zallinger, her son Peter is an illustrator, and one of her daughters, Kristina, is a painter and graphic artist. Mr. and Mrs. Zallinger live in North Haven, Connecticut.